D0067889

Love Knots

*How to Untangle Those Everyday Frustrations
and Arguments That Keep You from Being
Happy with the One You Love*

Lori Heyman Gordon

Illustrated by Mike Flint

The trademark PAIRS ® is registered in the US Patent and
Trademark Office.

ISBN: 0-44-0-50274-8

Printed in the United States of America
Published simultaneously in Canada

November 2011

10 9 8 7 6 5 4 3 2 1

Dedicated
to
VIRGINIA SATIR
beloved teacher, pathfinder, mentor, friend. She made this planet a more loving, more humane place.
and
MORRIS GORDON
my husband, whose unlimited vision makes possible the impossible and probable the improbable. His encouragement, patience, and love nurture and sustain me.

PREFACE

Lori Gordon, a talented psychotherapist, was inspired by one of her primary teachers, Virginia Satir. Satir was a remarkable pioneer who helped to develop the specialty of marital and family therapy. With her encouragement, Gordon began conceiving what developed into the PAIRS program. PAIRS is the acronym for PRACTICAL APPLICATION OF INTIMATE RELATIONSHIP SKILLS. Some years ago, I accepted Dr. Gordon's invitation to take her PAIRS program. In the training, a professional takes the same full course as others do. The course astounded me.

Dr. Gordon's genius lies in her ability to weave together a series of concepts and exercises. Many are her own creation, others are inspired by colleagues. She has taken from psychoanalysis, psychology, psychiatry and counseling programs the essence of their change producing techniques. She has organized them into a new entity that is far greater than the sum of its parts. Gordon has developed the PAIRS system into a synergistic force that helps individuals and couples find positive change to be relatively easy. It is serious and at the same time fun. After forty years of working with couples. I have found PAIRS to be my most important professional and personal tool. It is now being used extensively in this hemisphere, as well as in Europe.

LOVE KNOTS stands by itself. It is also an example of how Gordon's program works. It leads readers into an approach to themselves and others that is structured to resolve interpersonal conflict. The range of hidden expectations we have of ourselves and others that easily sabotage our most significant relationships, are illuminated with humor and poignancy through the LOVE KNOTS and DOUBLE BINDS.

Rarely do we read a book whose reverberating impact is capable of changing our lives or those of other people. The contents of this volume suggest that here is a way to improve important relationships without labeling anyone. Nor is this approach guilt provoking. In a sense, it helps us find ways to modify what may be maladaptive behavior today, but that was appropriate at earlier times in our lives. The text forestalls guilt and blame in a remarkable fashion, stripping away unnecessary defensiveness. An open collaborative process prepares us, as both individuals and couples, to evolve in our most significant intimate relationships, and to stand tall as we experience the changing world of the twenty-first century.

-Clifford Sager, M.D., Clinical Professor of Psychiatry, Payne Whitney Clinic Director, Marital and Family Outpatient Services, Cornell Medical Center

ACKNOWLEDGMENTS

To all those who joined me in identifying and untangling the knots in relationships and from whom I learned, I offer my deep appreciation. Special acknowledgment to Bill and Becky Bestimt. Bill claimed the entire collection as "the credo by which I live."

Special gratitude to Jon Frandsen for his clear editing, Mike Flint for his apt illustrations and Christy Allan Piper; Jean Milbradt, Pat Swift for their constant, caring administrative support. Sincere thanks for their many hours at the computer in making this work presentable. Deep appreciation to PAIRS leaders who recognized the potential of the knots and whose humor and insight further refined them.

Special thanks and love to my late parents Julius and Bertha Heyman, who encouraged my curiosity and puzzle solving, to my children Jon, David, Seth, and Beth; to Peggy (who dreamed up the title), Lisa, Fran, Maybelle, Selma, Arlene and Ami, and to my grandchildren Ronny, Donna, Guy, Jessica, Adam, Benjamin, Sara, Joshua, Alexander, Michael, Zachary, Lauren and Evan. May this list help you to avoid some of the pitfalls of love relationships.

CONTENTS

THE DOUBLE BINDS

INTRODUCTION

W e had everything going for us. How did we get to this?"

As a marriage and family therapist, I've spent many years reflecting on the puzzle of how initially loving, apparently intimate relationships so often suddenly founder and capsize. I found this puzzle to be comprised of many pieces, pieces that can be sources of misunderstanding and distress in relationships. The pieces formed a complex and rather colorful picture that evolved into my PAIRS (Practical Application of Intimate Relationship Skills) program. PAIRS is now a dynamic, comprehensive sixteen-week course that offers a guided series of exercises focused on those emotions, attitudes, and behaviors that nurture and sustain intimate relationships. It was developed and taught at the PAIRS Institute in Falls Church, Virginia, and elsewhere round the world. Since its beginnings, mental-health professionals from around the globe have trained to lead PAIRS programs.

As I developed the PAIRS program and investigated the intricacies of relationships, I found consistent, specific sources of trouble. These involve those hidden expectations and assumptions or beliefs that we bring to intimate relationships.

If we are unaware of our hidden expectations or the validity of our differences, they can, with surprising rapidity, sabotage and destroy our relationships. If our life experiences have conditioned us to defend ourselves against the vulnerability involved in love, trust, affection, confiding, closeness, and need, we develop defenses. Tony, a college professor who took PAIRS while well into his second marriage, wrote:

"I had such complicated defenses that I couldn't figure out the blueprints myself. The blueprints had been lost years ago and all that was left were the booby traps and fortifications, which had been there so long I thought they were part of the landscape."

The landscape of intimacy is littered with relationships that have been destroyed by hidden expectations and assumptions. Most couples who are unhappy in their relationship feel disappointed, if not outright betrayed, because what they expected to find in the relationship either hasn't happened or has stopped happening. It's as if they believe they had signed an invisible contract early on and their partner has failed to honor it. Sometimes, I learned as I conducted the early PAIRS courses, simply reading and recognizing hidden, unrealistic or faulty expectations makes it easier to reflect on them, and even laugh at and consider changing them.

Love Knots is one result of all this puzzling. It is a somewhat incomplete but often, I hope, helpful and humorous series of formulas designed to bring to the surface your hidden expectations of yourself and your partner. Awareness and reflection are powerful tools. It is my wish that this little book will help you to take that pause that will lead to new understanding, acceptance, and peace of mind.

May the list of knots and binds and the accompanying dialogue guide help you to avoid some of the pitfalls and find more of the pleasure possible between loving partners.

—Lori Heyman Gordon
Falls Church, Virginia

What Happened?

A simple caress from your husband feels like a sudden burn. You flinch and tell him to stop. You reach to hug your lover and he acts as if he's being sucked into a tremendous storm, yanking away without a word. You know by now that asking what's wrong just makes it worse and you leave the room. The house slowly divides into his-and-her territories, with the kitchen and bathroom serving as demilitarized zones. The bedroom is a quiet Twilight Zone, where temporary truces are called and broken over and over.

The thoughts during such times, sometimes spoken, sometimes kept hidden, are simple, sharp, and indisputable commands, ranging from a whispered and pained "Just leave me alone" to a furious "Go to hell." But when the enemy is gone and the threat has receded, you have time to think, not just react. Maybe you recall how much you loved to be touched or held by your partner, and begin to wonder how that same gesture came to mean something frightening, something that threatened to restrain or hurt rather than comfort. Maybe you fantasize about somebody else holding you in the same way. And maybe you just sit in the dark and let your brain shout one question over and over again, a question you might never ask the person with whom you share your life. "What happened?" What happened is you've been bumping into Love Knots and the even more tortuous Double Binds.

What's a Love Knot?

A Love Knot is caused by subconscious assumptions that we bring to our intimate relationships. It tends to act like a land mine—if touched, it explodes. It erodes relationships. It is based on our hidden beliefs and expectations, hidden from our partners and hidden from ourselves. We usually become somewhat aware of these beliefs only when we feel upset, angry, hurt, or disappointed. Even then we often don't know why.

We know we are withdrawing, either by shrinking away in pain from our partners or by chasing them off with anger. We know we just want to be away because our partners make us angry or feel hurt. But why?

Frequently we never find an answer to that question, and when we get tired of struggling to find it, we eventually shrug it off with a "Who knows" and "Who cares" and cope with the situation as best we can, either by letting it perpetuate or by leaving. We give up.

All of these expectations are based on hidden assumptions that we have developed through a lifetime, many of them faulty ones. Many of these beliefs have to do with talking about what we think or want. For example: "If you loved me, you would know what I think (feel, want)." The logic that follows is: "You don't, so you don't love me." Implicit here is the belief that if someone loves you, they know what's in your mind and heart and have an instinctive regard for your likes and dislikes. This isn't true. The only way to know for sure what someone wants or cares about is to be told. You must make your expectations explicit. To expect your partner to read your mind is to court disaster.

Another cluster of unhealthy assumptions has to do with expressing feelings: "If I tell you how I feel, you will be angry. I am afraid of your anger, so I can't tell you." Or: "If I tell you how I feel, you will be upset. I can't stand how I feel when you are upset, so I live a lie." Underlying these assumptions is the all too common but dead wrong belief that we are responsible for the way our partner feels. We are not. We are responsible for our own behavior and the way we express ourselves. We may try to avoid hurtful behaviors and expressions, but we cannot prevent those close to us from experiencing pain, fear, and anger. What we can do is listen when our partners want to express their feelings. Explaining those feelings allows them to diminish, and provides the information we need to talk about what caused the pain, fury, or fear. Then we can determine whether anything can be done about the cause.

We rarely ask ourselves why we expect certain things or particular behavior from the people we love. If we did, we might be surprised at some of the unfair demands we unconsciously make of our partners. And we might be surprised that we can indeed figure out "what happened." There are answers, and frequently the answers give us the tools we need to revive a relationship we desperately would like to count on and preserve. Identifying the hidden expectations each of us brings to a relationship is an important step toward resolving or warding off misunderstandings and disappointments. We expect things of intimates that we don't expect of anyone else. Our expectations become the basis of a private litmus test we constantly put our partners through without knowing it. They flunk when we experience a bewildering feeling of betrayal, when we realize that what we expected is not what our partners expected or are even capable of responding to.

The first key to finding out "what happened," or avoiding the alienation that tears many relationships apart, is ferreting out from our subconscious this list of faulty assumptions. Love Knots to which we subject ourselves and our partners. Once we identify those land mines, we can examine and reject them and replace them with positive attitudes and beliefs that allow us to grow closer to our partner, not run away.

Untangling the Knots and Using the Dialogue Guide

Read through the Love Knots and Double Binds in a thoughtful way. Don't be surprised if you find some of them disturbing. They may include beliefs you picked up so long ago, you may find it hard to believe they aren't simply truths. It may be difficult to imagine giving them up. Many of these messages are attitudes we developed while we were growing up, when other people controlled our lives and when we were trying to define, make sense of, and sometimes protect ourselves from the baffling ways in which adults behave. As you spot ones that fit, remember that they are worthy of respect; they helped you to cope with an ever-changing world. But now that we have greater control in our lives, we can develop new ways of coping with the world that allow us to explore its joys and secrets with fewer restraints.

Pay particular attention to the Love Knots and Double Binds that feel familiar. Try to think of situations where they may have hampered your relationship with a partner, family member, close friend, or even a colleague at work. Think through alternative ways in which you could handle those situations.

Each Love Knot (as well as the even more complex and convoluted Double Binds in the following section) is accompanied by a corresponding positive attitude that can be used to gently nudge out of the way the more destructive thoughts we carry with us.

In addition to habits of thinking that we develop from our earliest days, we also develop habits of expressing those thoughts. We have various styles we use to tell things to people and which have become deeply ingrained in the way we act. Unfortunately, many of those styles get in the way of what we are trying to say. The Dialogue Guide at the end of the book is a tool to help you understand and clearly express your concerns.

No matter what your beliefs, they're worthy of respect, as they enabled you to survive. Now, however, you want to live more fully and more joyfully.

The Love Knots

READ MY MIND!

If you loved me, you would
know what I think, feel, and want,
and you would give it to me.
Since you don't, you obviously don't care.

So why should I care for you,
or for what you think, feel, say, want, or do?
So when you tell me what you want,
I won't be interested.
I will be withholding.

I cannot assume that you know. I will ask for what
I want and not expect you to know.

WHO CARES?

If you loved me,
you would talk to me.
You don't.
You don't love me.

If you loved me,
you would listen to me.
You don't.
You don't love me.

Perhaps you're not a talker. Perhaps you are
preoccupied. Perhaps you never learned to talk
(or listen). I will check out my perceptions
and not assume.

IT'S MY STYLE

*If you loved me, you would
agree with me.
You don't.
You don't love me.*

*If you loved me, you would
want what I want and like what I like.
You don't.
You don't love me.*

*If you loved me, you would not
try to change me.
You try to change me.
You don't love me (for what I am).*

We are all unique. We are all different. Agreement
doesn't necessarily indicate love, nor does
disagreement necessarily indicate lack of love.
Differences can be discussed, understood,
changed, or accepted.

TAKE ME AWAY

If you loved me, you would bring excitement
and new experiences into my life.
You would plan them and make them happen.
You don't.
You must not feel I am worth doing that for.
You don't love me.

Part of our uniqueness is that
we are drawn to different things.
I must take responsibility myself
for making happen what I would like to have happen
and not see your initiative as a test
of my worth.

THE UGLY DUCKLING

*If you loved me,
you would find me attractive.
You would tell me so.
You would want to be close to me.
You don't.
You don't love me.*

**When you don't find me attractive, I cannot assume
I know why. I will ask for the information I need,
check out my perceptions, and not assume.**

LOSER FOR SURE

If you ask me to do something,
I'm afraid I won't do it well enough,
and that makes me feel inadequate.
So I don't do it at all.

Doing what I can because it pleases you is a gift to our relationship that nurtures love and trust. I don't need to be perfect. You are not my supervisor, judge, or parent, and I am not a child.

THANKS FOR THE MEMORY

If I were important to you,
you would remember what I tell you.
You don't.
You don't think what I have to say is important.
You don't think I'm important.
You don't love me.

My expectations are unrealistic. Even when you listen, you may be distracted, preoccupied, or forget. If what I want you to hear and remember is very important, I need to make you aware of it and get your full attention. Your ability to remember is not necessarily a reflection of your feelings for me. When I'm in doubt about your feelings, I will ask and not assume.

THE BIRTHDAY

If I were important to you,
you would remember special anniversaries,
special dates and times.
You don't.
I'm not important to you.
You don't love me.

When you don't remember these things, I will let you know their importance to me. I will tell you of my hurt, disappointment, or resentment. If you choose to ignore what is important to me, our relationship will surely suffer. We need to develop a relationship in which each of us feels loved and valued.

SEE NO EVIL

If you tell me what you want,
I feel controlled or obligated to do what you want.
When I feel controlled, I feel weak and inadequate.
I cannot give you what you ask for
without feeling resentful.

If you tell me your feelings,
I must do what you want.
That would interfere with what I want
(think, feel, am doing).
So I don't want to hear or know your feelings.

**We have to be able to report our feelings, and no
one is obligated to do anything about them.**

STINGY SANTA

If I give to you and you don't acknowledge it,
I feel unappreciated.
Since what I give you is unappreciated,
I will be withholding.

It is important to take pleasure in knowing that you are giving, without waiting to be acknowledged.

THE GILDED CHAIN

If I acknowledge how much you do for me,
I feel beholden, burdened, and obligated to do for you.
I don't want to, so I cannot acknowledge what you do.
You feel unappreciated.
You distance.

Expressing appreciation for what the other does is an important part of sustaining love. There is no obligation to return your partner's favors—that is your choice alone.

HEAVYWEIGHT CHAMP

If we don't agree,
one of us must be wrong.
If it is me, that means I am bad,
stupid, ignorant, or inadequate.
So it can't be me.
I must prove that it is you, so I won't feel like a failure.

We should be able to disagree.
We are all unique,
and disagreements are manifestations
of our uniqueness.

KEEPING UP WITH THE JONESES

If you are more successful, more competent, than I am,
I feel diminished and put down.
I distance myself from you.

**The only useful comparison is one with where you,
yourself, have been; what you are learning; and
what else you want to accomplish. Comparing
yourself to your partner evokes envy, jealousy, and
feelings of competition. We are all struggling to
survive and grow, to use the opportunities that life
offers to accomplish our goals. To sustain intimacy,
we need to offer each other mutual support and
encouragement.**

MASQUERADE

If I tell you how I feel,
you will be angry.
You will attack me or withhold from me.
I am afraid of your anger and your distance.
I can't tell you.
I live a lie.

If I tell you how I feel,
you will be hurt.
I can't stand how I feel when you are hurt.
I can't tell you.
I live a lie.

((LOVE))

We need to be able to risk confiding our feelings and to listen with understanding and empathy. We need to be able to listen to our partner's feelings, consider and discuss them. Acting out feelings by withholding, attack, or distance is destructive.

THE JUDGE

*If I tell you how I feel, you
interrupt, correct, give advice, judge, or dismiss my feelings.
I feel betrayed, angry, frustrated.
I won't tell you my feelings.
I distance.*

**If what I want is to be listened to and heard
without comment, I have to ask for that. Comments
are not welcome when what I want is for you to just
listen. We have to tell our partner what we want.**

**It is not a gift to give advice or comments when
they are not wanted or asked for. We need to be
able to listen for information and deeper
understanding. Listening is a most important gift to
the relationship.**

THE HANDYMAN

If you are in pain,
I feel I should be able to fix it.
I don't know how to fix it, so I feel inadequate.
I am angry at you for making me feel inadequate.
I withdraw from you, blame you,
when you are in pain.

When we're in pain, what we want is interest, comfort, empathy, sympathy, an interested ear, to be listened to—not solutions. As adults, we have our own intelligence and can figure out solutions for ourselves. If we want advice or help, we can ask for it.

ON YOUR OWN

If I were what I should be,
you would be happy.
I would be able to solve (fix) everything.
Since I can't, your unhappiness makes me feel
inadequate, guilty, angry—at you.
I distance myself from you.

**No one can solve or fix everything for another. No
one can take responsibility for another's happiness.
Each one must do that for himself or herself.**

PERFECTO THE INDESTRUCTIBLE

If I were what I should be,
I would never be weak, tired, inadequate, impotent, afraid...
But I am.
Therefore I feel inadequate.
I must hide my feelings
so you won't find out how inadequate I really am.
I live a lie.

All of us have times when we feel bad. Hiding our
feelings from each other keeps us strangers.
Sharing our feelings brings us closer.
Sharing your feelings helps your partner to be able
to confide his or her own feelings.

CHINKED ARMOR

If you were what you should be,
you would never be
sad, angry, bored, boring, worried, suspicious, tired,
loud, sick, selfish, weak, disagreeable, clumsy,
controlling, flirtatious, or demanding.
You are.
I feel cheated, betrayed.
I distance myself from you.

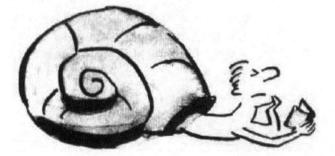

We are all different ways at different times. We each have many sides. We need to be able to accept this in each other and discuss the things we need changed when they're important to us.

IF ONLY

If you were what you should be,
I would be
happy, successful, popular, attractive,
virile, potent, sexy.
I'm not.
It's your fault.

No one can make the other be anything. It's up to each of us to work to develop those strengths and qualities we want for ourselves. We can ask our partner for help, but the responsibility for our destiny is ours.

HIDE AND GO SEEK

If I let you get close to me,
I fear I will be trapped, engulfed, or smothered.
I must keep my distance from you
and not allow you to get close.

Closeness can be an exquisite pleasure. As adults, no one can trap, engulf, or smother us, since we have our own power: to speak, to act, to leave if we so choose. It is important as adults to be able to be independent, to meet our separate needs; as well as interdependent, for closeness with and support from our partner.

PANDORA'S BOX

If I let you get close to me,
you will find out my secrets, my fears,
how inadequate I really am.
You won't love (respect) me.
I must keep you at a distance.

We are all lovable. We are all human. We feel closer when we can confide our secrets and fears to a caring, interested partner.

SAYS WHO?

If you say you love me,
you either don't know me,
want to use me, or are stupid
and have poor judgment.
I can't love you.

Life has risks. Relationships have risks. We all must choose whether to risk living with the pleasures or disappointments that may lie therein or to simply exist—without either. We will never know unless we try. As adults we have our own resources. We are not helpless, even when we are disappointed. We need to risk allowing ourselves to be known, check out our perceptions, and accept that we are lovable and good enough. Anyone who loves us has very good judgment.

OFF BALANCE

If I let myself get close to you,
I will need you.
If I am too dependent, need (love) you too much,
I will not be able to survive without you.
I will lose the ability to be alone,
to function on my own.
I will become weak.
I must avoid closeness,
I must distance myself from you, care less,
to be sure I won't miss (need) you too much
when you are gone (die, or leave me).

We can enjoy closeness yet still survive on our own if we need to. As adults we are not helpless, we can make new lives for ourselves if that's what life should require. The pleasures of intimacy are among life's most fulfilling gifts and are worth the risk of allowing feelings of need in order to enjoy intimacy when it can be there.

JUST SKIP IT

If I love you,
I will need you.
I cannot trust you to be there.
Therefore I cannot (will not) love you.

I'll decide for myself whether or not I can trust you,
based on my actual experiences with you—not on
my history or hidden expectations.

I KNEW IT

If I love you,
I will need you.
I do not trust you to stay.
I will provoke you, blame you, drive you away,
so that when you leave,
I will know
I was right.

The more I provoke you, blame you, drive you
away, the more you will feel uncared about and
have good reason to leave. And I will be responsible
for the fulfillment of my prophecy. Tests do not
create trust.

LOVE ME KNOT

I believe that:

A MAN should never be_____*	*A WOMAN should never be_____**
(irrational, illogical, weak, passive, sentimental, meek, incompetent, overwhelmed, tearful, wrong, embarrassing...)	*(demanding, selfish, unfeeling, aggressive, critical, too busy, bossy, angry, rational embarrassing...)*

If I am these things, I am defective.
I must hide, pretend, or wear a mask.

If you are these things, you are defective.
I feel betrayed.
You broke our contract.
I am entitled to belittle you, deceive you,
withhold from you, distance myself from you,
not love you.

We are all human. We all have moments of frailty, uncertainty, vulnerability, intensity. This does not make us defective. We need to be able to share ourselves with our partner and not hide.

*Add your own adjectives of imperfection and inadequacy.

ASS-U-ME

If you are distant from me,
you don't love me.
Therefore why should I love you?

I will ask and try to understand the reasons for
your distance. I will not assume.

The Double Binds

There are few things more frustrating than running across someone you never can please. If you act a certain way, he is suspicious; if you act another, she may act hurt or resentful. He is subjecting you to a Double Bind—a circular thought that can't be countered. If she doesn't change, you usually simply stop trying to please her. Or worse, he is so crazy making, you begin to doubt yourself and your own senses, constantly feeling inadequate.

The previous Love Knots are unhealthy beliefs because they translate into expectations that, while unfair or unrealistic, can be complied with. Double Binds, however, are more of a heads-I-win, tails-you-lose proposition that entraps our partners because there is no good way to resolve the situation. It's a no-win.

Consider this fairly common Double Bind: "If you give to me, I feel beholden, obligated, burdened . . . and I distance myself from you. If you don't give to me, I feel unloved, uncared for, unwanted."

Now wait a minute! How can anyone deal with two such strident and opposing thoughts? The only way a person having such a belief will ever be satisfied is to change, to learn to allow himself to enjoy being given to, to understand that true gifts do not come wrapped in obligation.

When you encounter a Double Bind in someone else, all you can do is gently point out the position in which you are placed. Since Love Knots and Double Binds usually are not conscious thoughts but attitudes that we act upon without thinking, your partner probably will be surprised when you draw attention to them. If you can point out the way such a thought affects you without blaming or attacking the other person, I hope he will appreciate the opportunity to make it easier for the relationship to thrive. If she displays no interest in changing, she has given you important information that will help you decide whether the relationship is worth the torment and crazy making that her Double Binds inflict upon you.

As you encounter Double Binds in yourself, don't despair. Until you recognize the irrational expectations that sabotage relationships, you can't begin to change them. Awareness is a powerful tool. You cannot change destructive attitudes until you know what they are.

NOW YOU SEE ME, NOW YOU DON'T

If I am attracted to you, I avoid you,
as I believe I am not good enough for you to be attracted to me.
If I am not attracted to you,
I can be comfortable and friendly, as I am not anxious.
I am always with the one I am not attracted to.

**I will take the risk of being with whom I am
attracted to and/or I will examine why I am not
drawn to those I am comfortable with. My attention
and interest are gifts. If they are not accepted, I may
be disappointed but I will survive. And perhaps I
will find myself with whom I actually want to be.
Perhaps not. I'll never know unless I risk it.**

HEADS YOU WIN, TAILS I LOSE

If I show you how much I love you and need you in my life,
my desire for you might drive you away,
so I never show you how much I care.
If I don't show you how much you mean to me and
how much I care,
you feel unloved and you distance from me.

**Showing love and caring to another are gifts. They
are not obligations nor need they be suffocation.
They are to be appreciated and enjoyed. If they do
not appear to be welcome, it is something to be
explored and discussed, not assumed.**

WHO CAN I TURN TO?

If you criticize me, I feel inadequate.
If you compliment me, you are placating or
controlling me,
by saying only what you think I want to hear.

**We need to be able to listen to, accept, and consider
both compliments and criticism, ask for clarification
if needed and decide what fits. We are all good
enough and lovable. We need to be able to trust
each other's honesty.**

TON OF BRICKS

If you need me, I feel obligated, pressured, burdened.
If you don't need me, I believe you don't care.

Your need does not obligate me. I know that as an
adult you have your own strength, resources, and
ability to solve problems. Your not needing me does
not mean you don't want or care for me. I can ask
and not assume.

SIMON SAYS

If I tell you what I want and you do what I want,
it doesn't count, because I had to tell you.

If I don't tell you what I want,
you don't do what I want.

If you do what I want,
but not the way I wanted you to,
it doesn't count.

I feel unloved.

I cannot expect you to know what I want, nor to do anything exactly the way I would. I can still appreciate the gift of whatever you do because you know I would like it.

OUT OF TOUCH

If I tell you what I want, you won't do it,
as you resent feeling controlled.
If I don't tell you what I want,
there's a slim chance you might do it,
so I NEVER tell you what I want.
After a while I stop even letting MYSELF
know what I want.
What do I want? I'm confused.

If I cannot tell you what I need or want, or how I feel, or what I think, I lose touch with myself. I must find a way to express myself and to tell you what I feel and want. If that is not possible and you don't want to know, perhaps we do not belong together.

IGNORANCE IS BLISS

If you tell me what you want,
I won't do it because
I resent feeling controlled.
If you don't tell me what you want,
then I may try to figure it out.
What do you want? I'll never know.

Giving you what you want is an act of caring that nurtures our relationship, pleasures you, and lets you know that I care. I need to be able to do this without feeling controlled or resentful. I can take pleasure in my ability to love.

GETTING YOUR WAY

If I agree to do what you want, and I do it well
you are getting your way and I resent that.
If I do it badly, I feel less than adequate.
I resent that.
I blame you. It's your fault that I'm upset.

When I keep my commitments, that is not you
getting your way. As an adult, I decide what
commitments I can make. When I keep them, I am
honoring my choices. That is part of being an adult.
Commitments allow each one to know what they
can count on. Honoring my commitments builds
trust and provides stability in a relationship.

MONKEY SEE

If I do what you want, and it's not what I want to do,
I resent it.
I believe you would resent it if I do what I want to do,
as it's not what you want to do.
So I never do what I want.
I'm miserable.
I hate you for making me miserable.

It is my choice alone and my responsibility to decide what I want to do and to do it, whether it is to please you or me. If I choose to do what pleases you, that is my choice and I will not resent it. I will take responsibility for my choices in doing those things that bring pleasure to my life whether you join me or not.

THE SERVANT

If I do what you want, you love me.
You only love what I do...not me.
I feel like nothing.
Therefore I will do nothing.

I will not assume you only love me if I do what you want. I will ask when I am in doubt.

GOTTA BE ME

If I am what you want me to be,
I dislike myself.
I resent you wanting me to be what I don't like.
If I am myself, you won't like me.
I resent you for not letting me be myself.

You are not responsible for my choices. They are mine alone. If we cannot work out expectations that we can accept and live with, then perhaps our differences are so great that we shouldn't be together. Perhaps they're not. We need to be able to talk about them.

HIDE AND SEEK

If you loved me, you would always want me with you.
If you want to be alone,
it means you don't want me with you.
If you always want me with you, I feel smothered.

All of us have times when we need to be separate,
and times when we enjoy and want to be together.
As adults, no one can always want to or always be
there for another. We have our separate lives to
lead, as well as those parts we share. These times
vary with each of us. We need to be able to accept
these differences and negotiate for the changes that
are important.

STRINGS ATTACHED

If you comfort (give to) me,
you are more powerful than I am.
I will not accept your comfort.
If I comfort you, you are comforted.
I resent you for being comfortable
when I never can be.

**Accepting comfort neither diminishes one nor
empowers the other; it should be a pleasure to give
and receive comfort from a caring partner. An
essential part of intimacy is accepting and
enjoying this.**

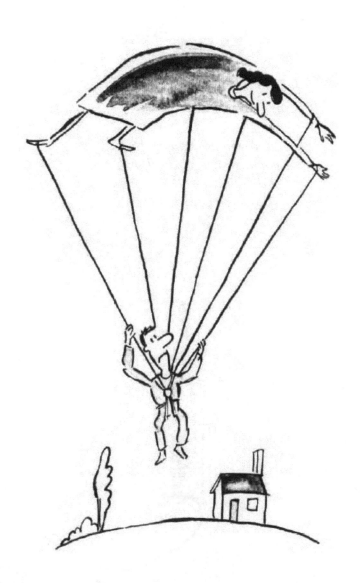

CONTENTS PRESSURIZED

If I tell you how I feel, you are angry.
If I don't tell you how I feel, you are angry.

If I tell you how angry I am at you,
you distance yourself from me.
If I don't tell you how angry I am,
I distance myself from you.

I need to be able to tell you my feelings and know you will try to listen with empathy. I also need to be able to accept and consider your responses and not assume I know in advance what they will be. We all change with time and new things we learn. We need to be able to discuss anything.

If I am angry,
I cannot tell you,
for you would . . . leave,
withhold from me, retaliate.
I am afraid to be without you. I am a coward.
I hate you for making me a coward.

You cannot make me anything. And I can survive without you if I have to. Some things are nonnegotiable.

ME AND MY SHADOW

If you don't love me, stay with me, I will die.
Therefore, I must cling to you no matter what the price.
The more I cling, the more you feel smothered and distance.
The more you distance yourself, the more I cling.

As an adult, I have my own power, my own strengths and resources. I may not want to, but I can survive without you. It is up to me to develop my strengths and resources to enable me to be self-sufficient enough not to have to cling.

THE PUSH-ME-PULL-YOU

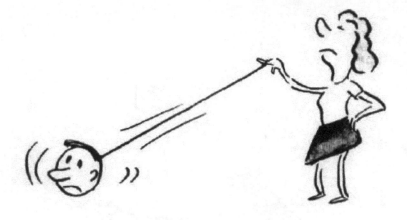

If I distance from you,
I miss what I have with you.
I draw closer.
If I need you, I am weak.
I hate myself for being weak.
I resent you for making me weak.
I distance myself from you.

Needing others is not a weakness. We all need each other, most certainly for bonding. Fulfilling this need happily is one of life's greatest pleasures. We miss it when we don't have it. When I need you, I don't lose my own strength. Each of us must work on our own history and early decisions that prevent us from experiencing and filling this need with pleasure.

BEAT IT

My commitment to you is too restrictive for me.
I wish to change it. I cannot tell you.
You would be upset.
To see you is to experience my guilt.
I will find reasons to be angry with you,
so I need not feel guilty.
I will provoke you, anger you, drive you away,
to give me a reason to be angry with you . . .
so I can feel justified in my behavior,
in breaking my commitment,
and not feel guilty.

Relationships change through time. What may have worked at the beginning changes as we grow and our situations change. My desire to be with others need not be a rejection of you but an expression of my own need for variety, new experiences, and the richness of a range of relationships in my life. My ability to be separate from you and enjoy other people and experiences has the possibility to enrich our relationship when we are together. Neither one of us needs to feel guilty about altering our original expectations. Renegotiating expectations, so long as this is not done unilaterally or arbitrarily, is ongoing and needs to encompass change in order to maximize mutual pleasure in fulfilling each of our evolving needs and goals.

And yet I love, need, want you, ...

As you examine the preceding Love Knots and Double Binds
and discover things that may feel uncomfortably familiar, try
to avoid the all too common human reaction of berating
yourself or finding fault. Instead, congratulate yourself for
discovering things that sabotage relationships and that you
can change. Become a detective with your partner and
compare lists and help identify some of each other's hidden
assumptions.

By acknowledging some of the silly or damaging things we believe, we can laugh at them together. Then we can, in an air of mutual trust and honesty, replace them with more livable, human beliefs that allow those we love to know what we want or expect and give them and ourselves a fair chance to meet those expectations.

The Dialogue Guide

In the preceding pages you've seen how, at least on a basic level, an awareness of, and then a subtle shift in a long-held attitude, can make a big difference in your relationships. But how do you carry those attitude shifts into real-life situations?

When you don't assume or expect unreasonably, your conversations will become much less full of blame and accusation. More attention probably will be paid to explanation and understanding. And sometimes understanding can begin with talking. Awareness can be teased out in many ways. Clear and direct, sometimes even blunt conversations, free of accusations and presumptions, can help a troubled relationship greatly.

This isn't easy, though, and that's what this section is all about. Many of us find talking about issues that can cause conflict very difficult. We grow angry or fearful and defend ourselves by lashing out or avoiding the issue.

For instance: Susan and Jim have three grown children, all of whom live in different states. Jim is content to stay in touch with occasional letters and visits, restricting long-distance calls to brief, businesslike conversations or problem-solving sessions. But Susan likes to talk to each of her children at least every week or two, maybe more often, because it makes her feel good to stay in touch and share little things—perhaps a joke or a fond memory or maybe even a tidbit of family gossip. This drives Jim wild. To him, long-distance calls are to exchange essential information, not to make unnecessary conversation.

When Susan spends more than five or ten minutes on the phone, more likely than not he will begin to pace where she is sitting, glancing at his watch while he fumes. She may just turn her back to him and try to ignore him, or she might snap at him, saying, "Just five more minutes."

After a particularly long call, during which Jim has spent the last ten to fifteen minutes interrupting and just hovering around, Susan decides to deal with the issue.

"Why were you such a pain in the neck while I was on the phone?" she asks.

"Because I can't stand watching you throw money down a rat hole. I have no intention of supporting the telephone company. I swear, I think you do that just to aggravate me."

"Money isn't the issue. You spend more every week on new tools you never use than I do on the phone. You resent me being so close to the children. It's not my fault you never tried to keep up with your own kids."

At this point, Jim either explodes and makes an accusation of his own and the argument turns into lengthy antagonism, or he just withdraws and refuses to discuss the matter further. Nothing gets resolved. Instead, more touchy issues, sore points, and grudges get brought up, and soon all that is left are open wounds with no bandages in sight. What starts out as a simple, if cranky, question strays quickly into a number of unrelated areas as each partner tries to outscore the other and "win."

It might not be easy for Susan and Jim simply to take a look through the Love Knots in this book and resolve all the issues that prompted this argument (although it would get them on the right track). Susan and Jim need to talk. They need a way out that is specific to them.

If Susan reads through the list of Love Knots and Double Binds, she might discover that one of her hidden assumptions is "If you loved me, you would know what I want" (in this case, to stay in touch with her kids by phone).

Further, she may also have a rule about anger: "If I tell you how I feel, you will be angry. I am afraid of your anger, so I don't tell you." So with those two hidden assumptions, Susan has boxed herself in. Every time she's on the phone for a long period of time, she ends up feeling unloved, angry, and defensive. When she could take a few minutes to explain why this bothers her so much, she's afraid to and decides to skip it. So instead of making her feelings clear, she uses a heated moment to lash out and blame Jim, who lashes out himself and blames her.

Going through the Love Knots might help Susan and Jim gain a greater understanding of how certain private rules and beliefs might get in the way of their relationship, but they still need to clear things up between them. They need to talk things through in a way that can better ensure that the point is not obscured by assumptions about each other, concerns about power and who wins the argument or apprehensions about how the other will respond. We often take those closest to us for granted, expecting things of them we would never expect of a casual acquaintance, such as the ability to read our minds; or we "read" their minds, assuming that we know them so well, we know right away that "what you really mean is . . ." And often we are wrong. So what we need to do is tell our partners what we feel and think in a way that does not threaten them but gives them an opportunity, in turn, to explain clearly and honestly what they think.

The only thing we should expect in such a conversation is that each will attempt to understand the other, listening carefully and with empathy.

The accompanying Dialogue Guide helps provide a structure for such non-threatening conversations. Because we are sometimes only vaguely aware of what may be upsetting us, the Dialogue Guide provides starter sentences that are arranged to help you discover and sort out your perceptions, thoughts, and feelings. The idea is to share information, to say, in effect: "What I tell you will be my truth, and then you can tell me what meaning it has for you."

As an example, using a different issue, rather than attacking Jim, Susan could try to resolve it by using the Dialogue Guide. The result would look a little like this:

I NOTICE (behavior) . . . that whenever I try to tell you something I'm upset about, you interrupt, give me advice or walk away.

I ASSUME (this means) . . . that you think I need advice, or you're not interested when I'm upset.

I WONDER . . . why you react this way.

I SUSPECT . . . that you think you have to fix everything that bothers me and that you're trying to do that or you lose interest.

I THINK . . . that I should be able to tell you things that bother me, even when they're not about you, or even if they might be about you.

I RESENT . . . your not taking the time to listen to me and to care about what I'm feeling.

I AM PUZZLED BY . . . why you do this.

I AM HURT BY . . . your not wanting to know or listen to what I'm feeling.

I REGRET . . . that I can't confide in you about the things that upset me.

I AM AFRAID (based on past experience) . . . that if you keep doing this, it will cause me to stop telling you what I'm feeling.

I AM FRUSTRATED BY . . . this happening, when I've mentioned before that it bothers me.

I BEHAVE BY ...stopping talking to you about anything.

I AM HAPPIER WHEN ... I can tell you what I'm feeling and you don't judge it and just want to know.

I WANT . . to be able to talk to you when I'm upset about something and you just listen, and perhaps even put your arm around me. And ask me if I want to know what you think about it. Maybe I don't.

I EXPECT (this will help us by) . . . my feeling closer to you and much more loving.

I APPRECIATE . . . how much fun we have together, and how many things you do to help.

I REALIZE . . that you don't like to see me upset. But I want to be able to talk to you about everything because you're my best friend.

I HOPE . . . my telling you can help us. It's very important to me.

Take a few minutes to study the Dialogue Guide and think of one issue. How would you finish the sentence stems? To get a feel for using the Dialogue Guide, start with a relatively trivial complaint, such as, "I notice that I always seem to have to remind you to take out the garbage". Pick an issue on which you do not feel fully understood. As one person begins, the other should listen to what's being said with empathy, interest, and for understanding.

The listener may not interrupt with advice, rebuttal, judgments, or comment. After each point, the listener mirrors back what they heard, changing pronouns for accuracy [i.e., "I notice that you..." becomes "You notice that I..."]. If significant parts are missing, or there has been a misunderstanding of what was said, the speaker just repeats those parts, and the listener mirrors them back.

At the end of the Dialogue Guide the listener should show their appreciation for being taken into their partner's confidence with a gesture like a hug or a kiss. This step is essential before he goes on to take his turn, in which he can either respond to his partner's issue or raise one of his own. Make sure that each partner takes a turn using the Dialogue Guide. It doesn't matter who goes first.

The beauty of the Dialogue Guide is that it helps you to be very specific about issues that have felt vague. Although the Dialogue Guide may strike you or your partner as a silly or artificial structure, ask yourselves if you are satisfied with the way you currently discuss and deal with touchy issues. Time and again it has contributed to increased understanding of troublesome issues and helped to resolve them.

This guide is merely a model, a reminder that these various thoughts and feelings exist and that they affect your expectations and your behavior. You can, when you choose to, become aware of them so as to have a broader base of understanding with each other. As you grow more comfortable and familiar with a sequence of observations and feelings, you may want to tailor it so it better fits your own needs, changing the order of sentences, subtracting or perhaps adding your own sentence stems. You may want to ask: "How does this feel for you?" or "How can we work this out?" However, it won't do you any harm to practice the Dialogue Guide for a while in the sequence suggested, realizing that everything in the sequence can be of value in developing deeper levels of understanding for yourself and your partner. It can even be of help in simply collecting your thoughts and feelings at any point in time.

Now, with the list of Love Knots as a road map, and the Dialogue Guide as a compass, you have new tools to use with your partner to help identify some of each other's hidden assumptions and expectations and how to avoid problems that neither of you need!

DIALOGUE GUIDE

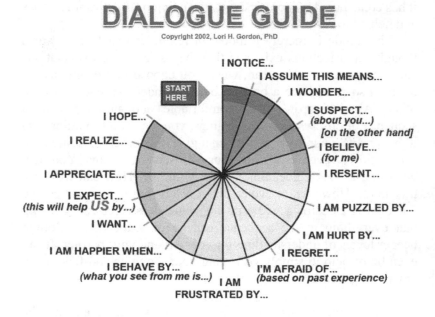